An Evening
at The Intersection
with
Poet Margie Steiner

Poems
Margie Steiner

Illustrations by
Claire Fraschina

Edited by Natalie Galli

Design & Production
Philip DiLernia

ISBN: 978-0-9973862-2-6

SUNBATH STUDIOS
SAN FRANCISCO
CALIFORNIA

756 Union Street

During her teen years through her early twenties,
San Francisco native Margie Steiner wrote the
poems presented in this collection.
On April 11, 1978, she read them all to a live
audience at The Intersection in North Beach.
Home to the legendary Pitschel Players
improvisatory group, The Intersection
at 756 Union Street celebrated
San Francisco's art, theatre,
dance and literary riches with
performances open to the public.

For Margie's husband,
Maxey McClintock

Margie Steiner's Poems

Margie Steiner's Word Collages

Recent Discoveries

Margie Steiner's Poems

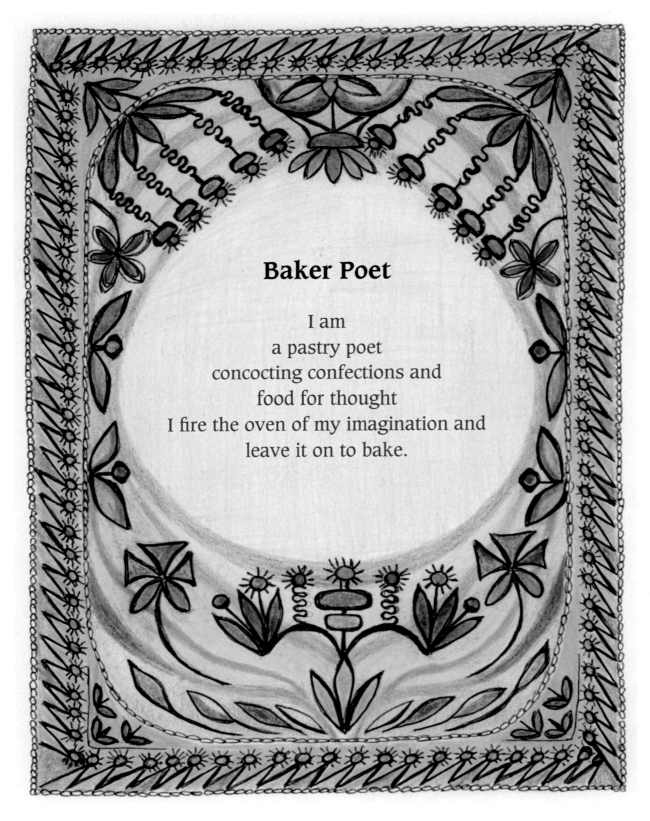

Baker Poet

I am
a pastry poet
concocting confections and
food for thought
I fire the oven of my imagination and
leave it on to bake.

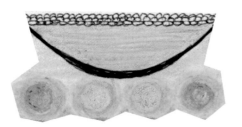

My Poems

My poems
are me
lying outside on
sheets of Saharan paper
sunbathing nude.

On a Winter's Day

To feel you breathe
to see you take in cold air
and send it out
warm again
on a crisp and
crinkly kind of day.

Mosses I Lichen

Chlorophyllic filaments
of elemental green essence
joining hands
Plant love.

Oyster

An alchemist underwater
unknown in her oceanic cave
shuts herself away with a grain of sand
philosophizing about beauty
in the outwardly ugly

Over time she offers
a silver-hued pearl

The illustrious globe of nacre
is not the Soul
but the alchemist
the oyster shucked
parted from her shell
her mollusk body dropping
Is.

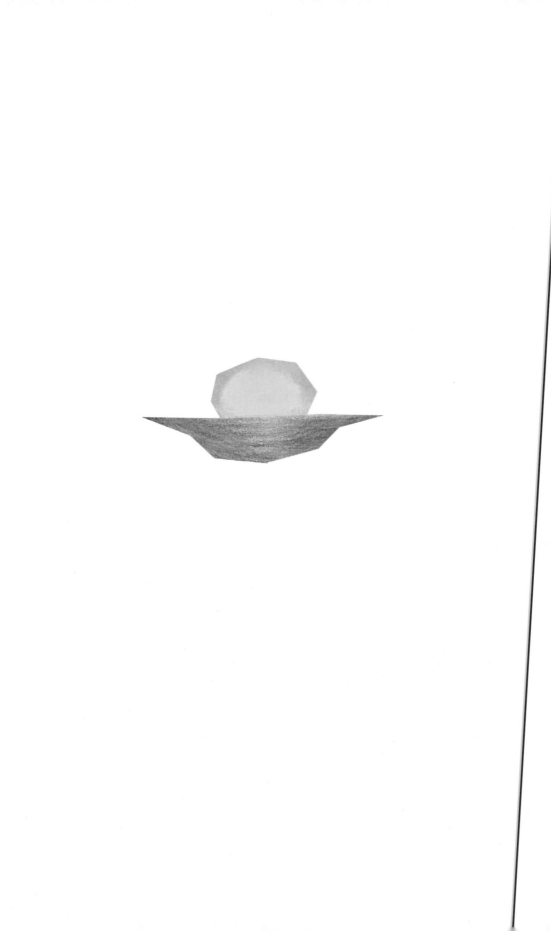

Sun Set At Sea

Lowered slowly on an unseen chain
an amber ember-sphere
celestial pendant
rests on the horizon
Becoming a serene cerise
the sun set at sea
is Apollo's gift to me
Becoming silky gilt sea
the Nereids swallow Apollo
The sun set at sea
is Neptune's gift to me.

Observation

A lone Monterey cypress
set apart
peers down at the
waves trying to reach her roots
and draws deeper within
wind-sculpted trunk
twisted in torturous curves
lined with worry and grey.

Supple sea surf
splashes toward
her brittle branches
she bristles stiffly
grey-green limbs
no longer
bending and swaying
dying on Yin Yang peninsula.

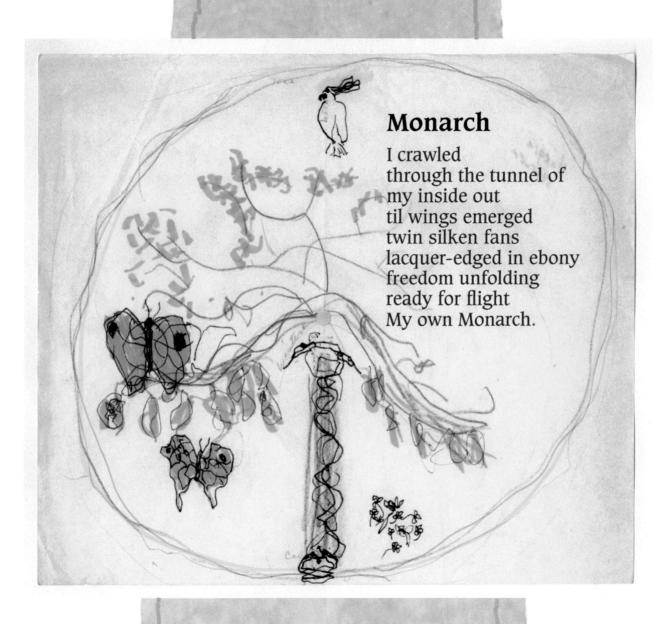

Monarch

I crawled
through the tunnel of
my inside out
til wings emerged
twin silken fans
lacquer-edged in ebony
freedom unfolding
ready for flight
My own Monarch.

Moving

My legs were blind and
my soul ached to transcend
the torment of its mortal casement
metaphysically climbing trees
to drink wind and sun
into my thirsty being
let country's golden energy
revitalize my stripped mines!

I moved
to another
place in time
to see past
previous hills
and mountains
to further peaks.
My travels have been
through Peoples Parks
I walked right out of Berkeley
to challenge
the city
and watched
the redwoods grow
twenty feet taller as
twilight filtered in.

I searched the night skies
for life light
A solar sparkler from distal regions
appeared alone, twirling silently
revolving with infinite swiftness
expanding multiplying dividing into
stellar cells of white light
The flicking signals,
the light starlight,
reaping celestial scents
left by a cosmic scythe,
poured down
from heaven to me.

A silver-capped wave
at Big River Mendocino
heading for firm land
sank into sandy layers
Pulled by the moon
it swelled each time
landing further ashore
quiet atop a sandbar
of golden bliss
unseen stars twinkling
in the sky high above.

However Pelucid

Illusion comes
cloaked with the
darkness of night
covering the bare arms
of the unseen
the unknown
Our gaze riveted upon
the shifting
the shimmering
cape of Morgana Fata
Unveiling her embrace
beckoning
beguiling
she spreads across
our horizons
Enmeshed in webs
we spin and
do not see
our weaving
However sheer the sheath
we must catch hold
the gossamer threads.

At Midday

On my back I lay
floating beneath an aqua blue sky
palm trees waved their wand-like fronds
and offered their friendship
peacefully summoning me
to higher planes
The reflections on the pool
so completely still
I could not be sure whether
the water lilies had achieved
a perfect lotus position
or were doing yoga
on their heads
Floating above a cielo blue pool
palm trees
peacefully summoned me
to higher places
upside-down, reflected places.

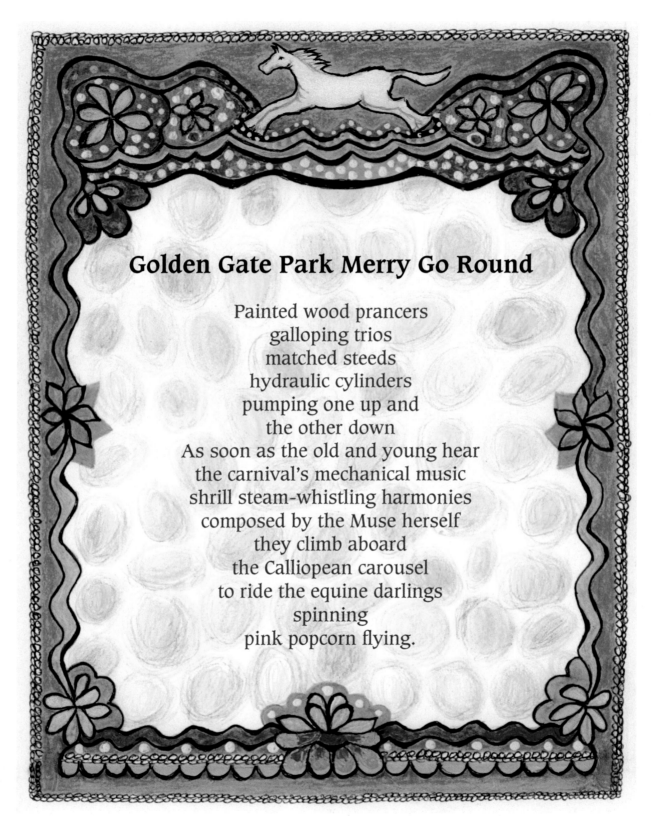

Golden Gate Park Merry Go Round

Painted wood prancers
galloping trios
matched steeds
hydraulic cylinders
pumping one up and
the other down
As soon as the old and young hear
the carnival's mechanical music
shrill steam-whistling harmonies
composed by the Muse herself
they climb aboard
the Calliopean carousel
to ride the equine darlings
spinning
pink popcorn flying.

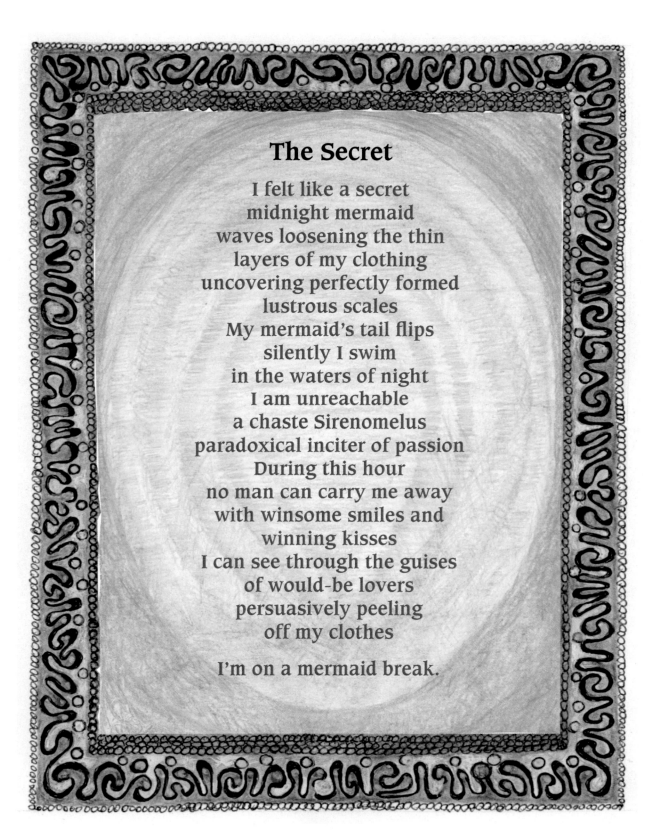

The Secret

I felt like a secret
midnight mermaid
waves loosening the thin
layers of my clothing
uncovering perfectly formed
lustrous scales
My mermaid's tail flips
silently I swim
in the waters of night
I am unreachable
a chaste Sirenomelus
paradoxical inciter of passion
During this hour
no man can carry me away
with winsome smiles and
winning kisses
I can see through the guises
of would-be lovers
persuasively peeling
off my clothes

I'm on a mermaid break.

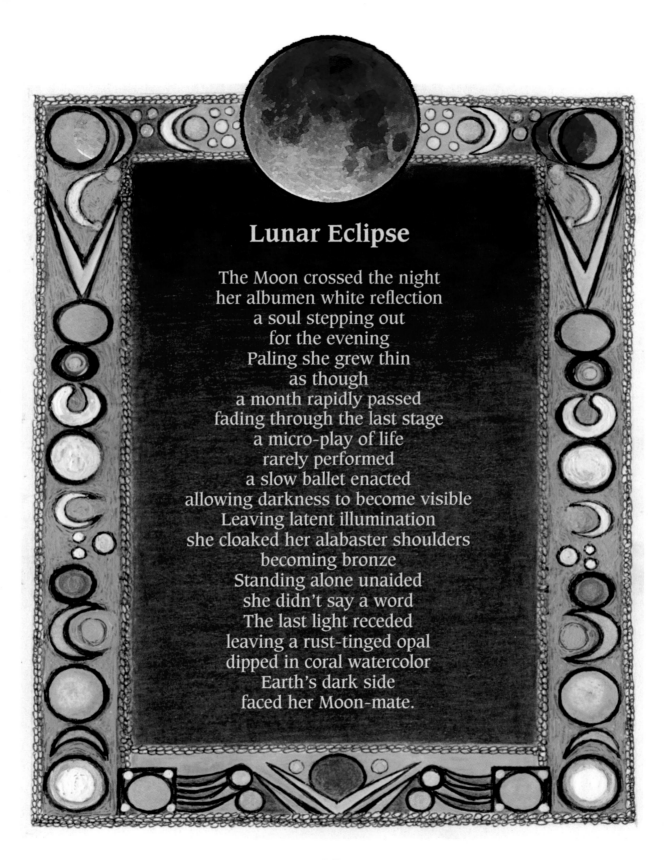

Lunar Eclipse

The Moon crossed the night
her albumen white reflection
a soul stepping out
for the evening
Paling she grew thin
as though
a month rapidly passed
fading through the last stage
a micro-play of life
rarely performed
a slow ballet enacted
allowing darkness to become visible
Leaving latent illumination
she cloaked her alabaster shoulders
becoming bronze
Standing alone unaided
she didn't say a word
The last light receded
leaving a rust-tinged opal
dipped in coral watercolor
Earth's dark side
faced her Moon-mate.

Anniversary

My heart has the sniffles
neither a perfect pink
marble case
with gilded sides
nor a silver locket
will cure it,
Sweetheart
You aren't my owner
you can't just
change the records
You think yourself master?
I am no Pandora
I am no Greek bearing
false gifts
I wear no padded brassiere
no gleaming enameled teeth
bridging gaps
I am no Jelly Roll
with gold fillings
reddened cheeks blushing
or eyebrows written in
I wear no platinum fall
cascading to the floor
I carry no lidless box
of ills and woe
Crying teardrops
carved out of the centuries
that women
have suffered
does not harden
my heart
Hand me that hanky,
Sweetie.

Black Bear at Twain Harte

Six girls' toes pushing
through warm sand
the sunlight watching
over young bodies shining
Six girls equipped
with unbreakable cups
from the cabin rental
searching for tadpoles
among the reeds
at the summer lake
Five hundred pounds of California
raced up the trunk of a Sierra pine
to observe the scene
Four thousand three hundred and
twenty red ants
going about the business
of maintaining their
underground colony
One Dad swimming to the big boulder
Zero problems for six girls.

Summer Solstice

I am the Sun.
For half a year now
I have climbed steadily
ascending the steps of an invisible pyramid
leading up the pathway of the celestial
sphere
to reach my apex and
bring to you
the first day of summer!
I am visiting the stellar home of Heracles
With my constant stride
I cover magnitudes of distance
appearing effortless
I glide with great force
thrusting myself forward twelve miles
every second brings me
closer to zenith.

Have you seen me?
On this, the longest day
of the year
I stand at full height
rejoicing.
During my eternal quest
I do not stop to rest.
Daily I sow unseen fields
above the Earth
with seeds of light
sprouting at dawn

a sapphirine savannah
As I cross the threshold
leaving spring behind
I carry you with me
rejoicing in the summer solstice
I summon you
to join with me
in celebration
I beckon.

I am the Sun
Goddess Arinnitti of Arinna
I am your divine ancestress
the many-named Golden One.
Call aloud for Arinnitti and
I will journey
from the ancient land of Hatti
I will rise
from the bower of night
to answer your prayer.
I bring to you
bouquets of heliotrope,
luxuriant in her growth
of bronzed green leaves and
circular clusters of deep purple
musky lilac fragrant flowers.
Where I point my finger rays
goldenrod grows,
ripening into wand-like boughs.

Warbling musical poetry to her lover,
The yellow-breasted phoebe
announces my appearance
as she dances,
hopping from branch to branch.
You may catch a gilded glimpse of me
filtering through the trees,
for my ever-pregnant belly
belies my presence with
the intense brilliance
of my searching light.
I am a swiftly spinning star
the radiant source of life.

Have you seen Kushuh?
When the last of Hours,
like the youngest of twelve dutiful sisters,
has bowed and taken her leave,
when I have draped myself
in velvet black and
entered the unlit tunnel
to the underworld,
You will see Kushuh,
God of the Moon,
Shhsh. If you look carefully,
you will discover
the winged figure of the lean one,
gracefully balanced,
his feet planted sturdily

on the shoulders of a lion.
If you do not find his
dim outline,
your eyes will catch the gleam from
the lunar crescent of his bronze helmet.
Only his emblem shows as
he guides the oars
through the blue reeds of dusk.
Kushuh, Kushuh;
openhearted and unpretentious,
his strength rules a thousand tides,
his power is unequalled.

As I leave behind day and
you feel the warmth
of my passionate love
and my daughters' vision and illumination
receding
Kushuh, god of the moon receives me.
Keeping my crown of rays
safely until I return,
he reflects light
with his penetrating beam
he speaks as you sleep
he hews a flickering
foot path for vision
to wend his way to
your door
with his basket of dreams.

Rise like the Sun and
seek out my warmth.
Come with me on this day
as we cross the threshold
leaving spring behind.
I carry you with me
rejoicing in the summer solstice
I summon you
to join with me
in celebration
I beckon.

I am the Sun.
In the later years,
there were those who forgot me,
the Sun
Goddess
Arinnitti of Arrina.
There were those who drove away my believers,
knowledge of me temporarily buried
with their bones
The Sun
Goddess
Arinnitti of Arrina
light entombed
with her ancestral sisters and brothers,

The Sun
Goddess

Arinnitti of Arrina
temporarily buried
with our celestial sisters and brothers.

For a few centuries
you may only have known of me
As Egypt's Sun god Re.
Once again I appear before you
I am the Sun
Goddess
Arinnitti of Arrina
I am your divine ancestress,
the many-named Golden One.
Riding the crest of heaven
I am lifted up by the Goddess Nut
She supports my sphere-shaped body
atop her head
I light worlds below me.
At the start of day
you will find the sovereign of Heaven
at sea level
Goddess Nut kneels
holding her arms outstretched
wings sprout fully from her golden limbs
feathers diffracting my solid being
diffused into shimmery sunshine.
At the close of day
as I descend the steeply graduated
terraces of time

you will discover the Goddess Nut
- this Lady of the High Place -
balancing gracefully.
Held aloft by Shu,
foundation of the sky
Lord Air raises his arms
cradling his celestial daughter
as she arches over the horizon
Goddess Nut,
This lady of the High Place,
cradling me in her softness
gently caressing me
her wing tips
tenderly stroking you
her wing tips
radiating my warmth entering you
I am the Sun God Re
I am the Sun Goddess Arinnitti
radiating my warmth touching you
radiating my warmth healing you
reaching out
I am the Sun Goddess Arinnitti
rejoicing in the Summer solstice
I summon you
to join with me
in celebration
I beckon
I am the Sun
for a year
I have climbed.

The Pyramid of Life

```
        love o Life!
        love ooo life!
       love ooooo life!
      love ooooooo life!
      love ooooooooo life!
     love ooooooooooo life!
     love ooooooooooooo life!
    love ooooooooooooooo life!
    love ooooooooooooooooo life!
   love ooooooooooooooooooo life!
   love of life o love o life o love!
   love ooooooooooooooooooooooo life!
  love ooooooooooooooooooooooooo life!
  love to peer amid life oooooooooo life!
 love oooooooooooooooooooooooooooooo life!
 love ooooooooooooooooooooooooooooooo life!
 love oooooooooooooooooooooooooooooooooo life!
 love ooooooooooooooooooooooooooooooooooo life!
love oooooooooooooooooooooooooooooooooooooo life!
love ooooooooooooooooooooooooooooooooooooooo life!
love oooooooooooooooooooooooooooooooooooooooo life!
love ooooooooooooooooooooooooooooooooooooooooo life!
love oooooooooooooooooooooooooooooooooooooooooo life!
love the pier amid life oooooooooooooooooooooooooo life!
love ooooooooooooooooooooo life's water oooooooooooooooooo life!
love oooooooooooooooooooooooooooooooooooooooooooooooo life!
love ooooooooooooooooooooooooooooooooooooooooooooooooo life!
love oooooooooooooooooooooooooooooooooooooooooooooooooo life!
love the pyre amid life ooooooooooooooooooooooooooooooooooo life!
love oooooooooooooooooooooooooooooooooooooooooooooooooooo life!
```

The Snow Queen

Gliding aloft
a giant snow goose
outstretched I lay atop her wings

Soft sojourners
flowing with peaceful
air currents
high above the snow-covered land
I have never known

Tucked in her feathery down
nestled midair
without a care
of weight

Looking out over the edges of
her feathers fluttering
riding slow motion into
the great white wonderland
drifting into
I drift within sleep.

Margie Steiner's Word Collages

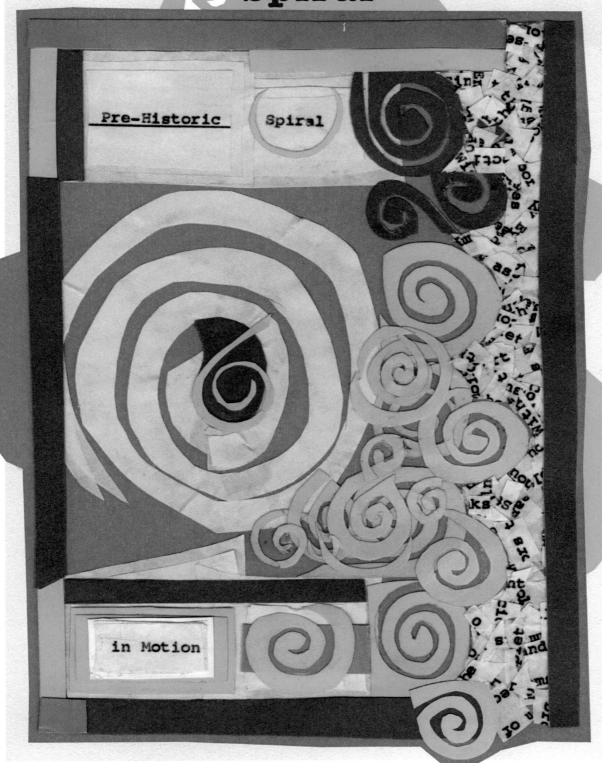

Pre-Historic   Spiral

in Motion

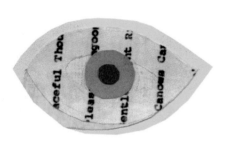

Golden Friend

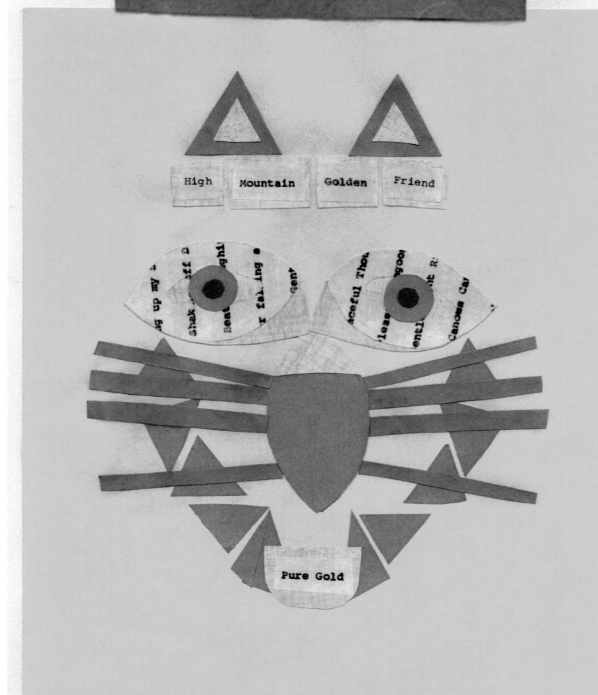

High Mountain Golden Friend

Pure Gold

Gentle Night Rides

Shaking off Day-Time

Drum Beats

Enter

Canoes

Pleasant Lagoons

Lakes   Streams   Ponds

Water Falls

Hear the Owl Hoot ▶ Love

Sunlight

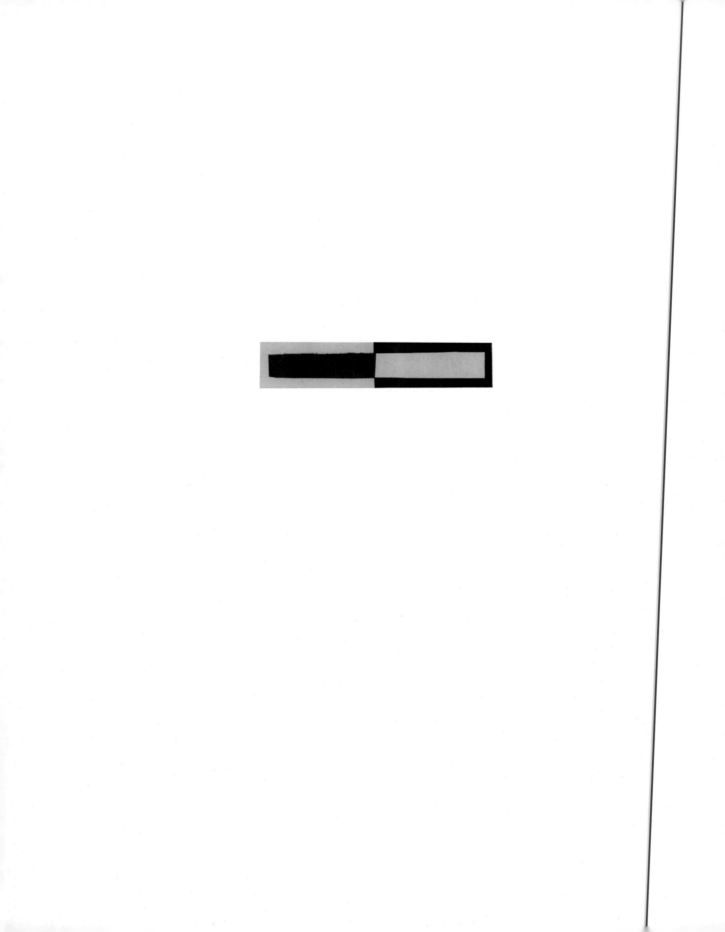

the Full Moon beams

Dust of Gold

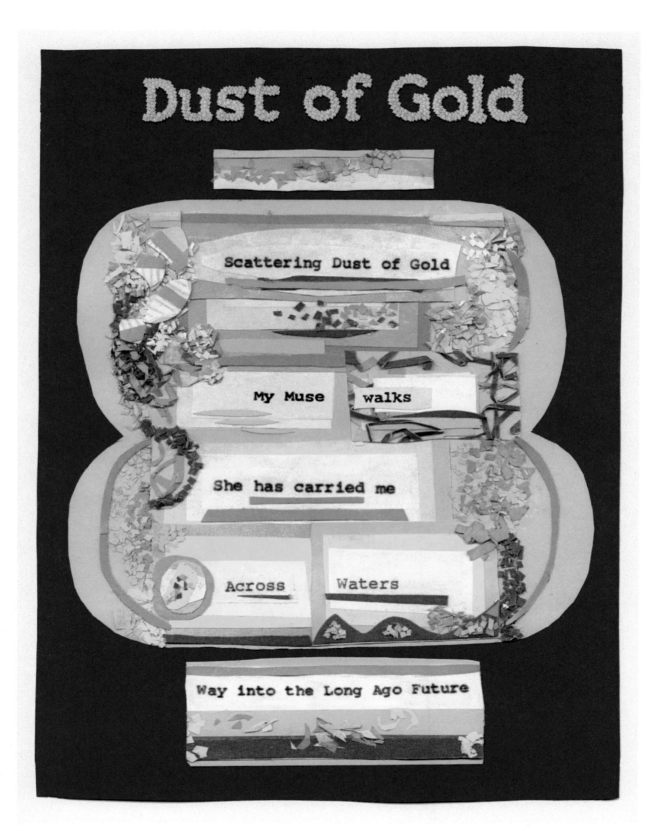

Scattering Dust of Gold

My Muse walks

She has carried me

Across Waters

Way into the Long Ago Future

Leaf Light

Light

Leaf
Light

Light

Light

Light

Plant's Finger Tips

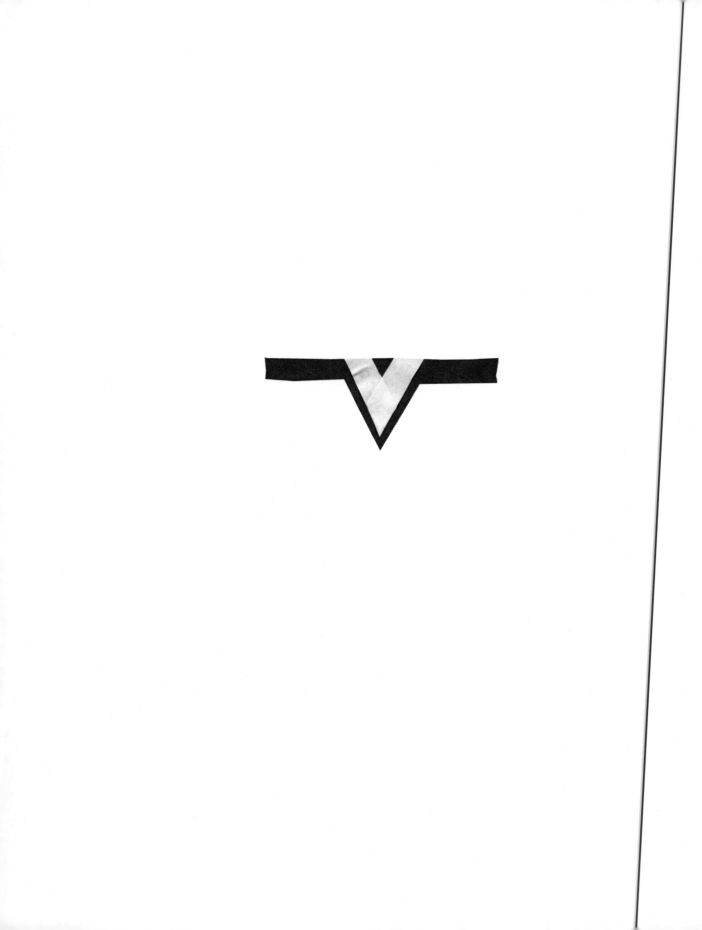

Vapor

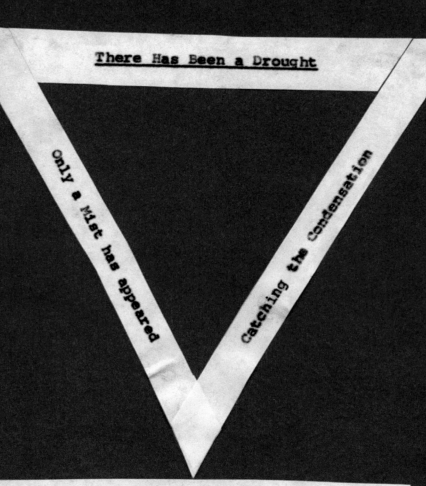

There Has Been a Drought

Only a Mist has appeared

Catching the Condensation

Hymns were Heard in the Roar of the Vapor

Air Bubble

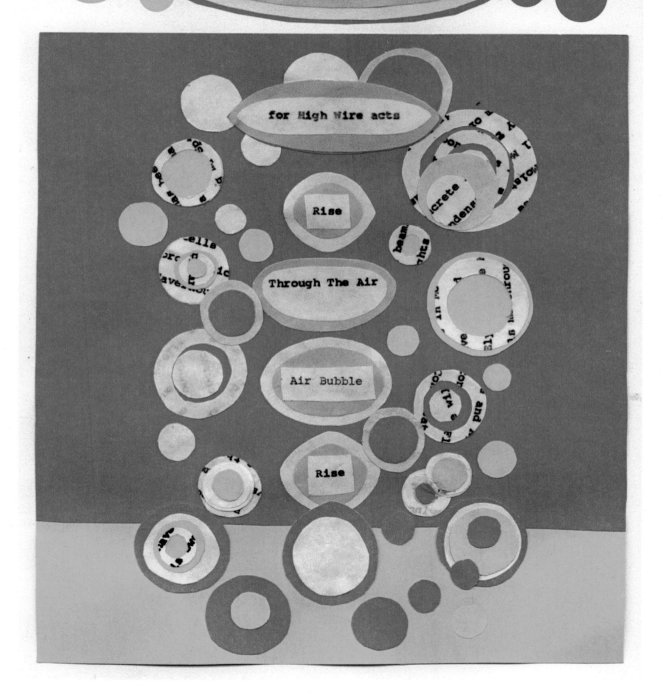

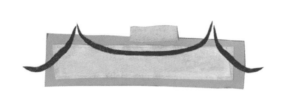

The Golden Gate

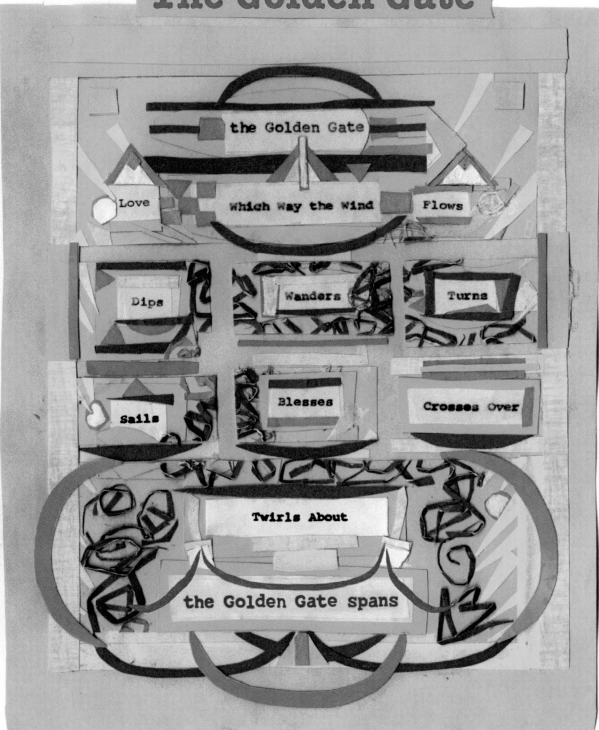

the Golden Gate

Love   Which Way the Wind   Flows

Dips   Wanders   Turns

Sails   Blesses   Crosses Over

Twirls About

the Golden Gate spans

Peak

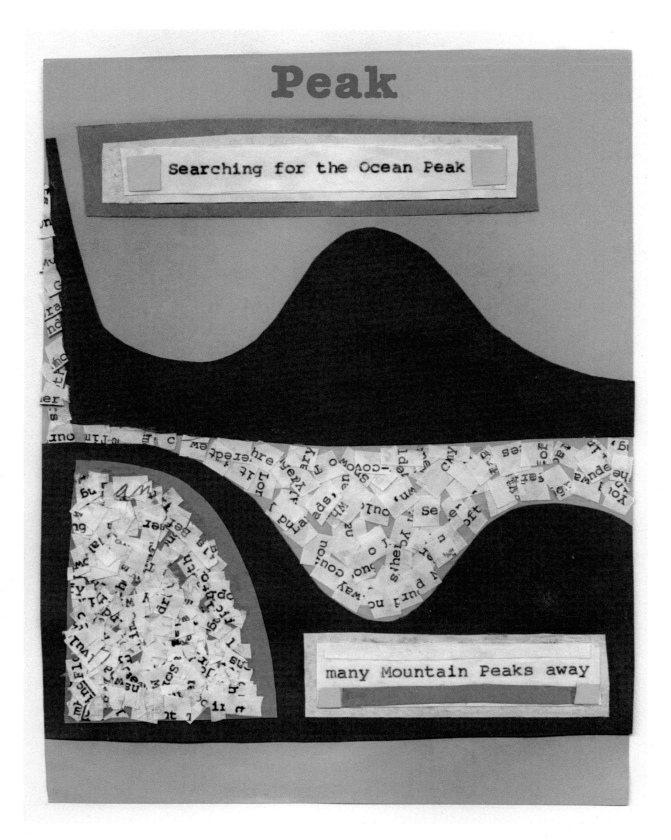

Searching for the Ocean Peak

many Mountain Peaks away

Love

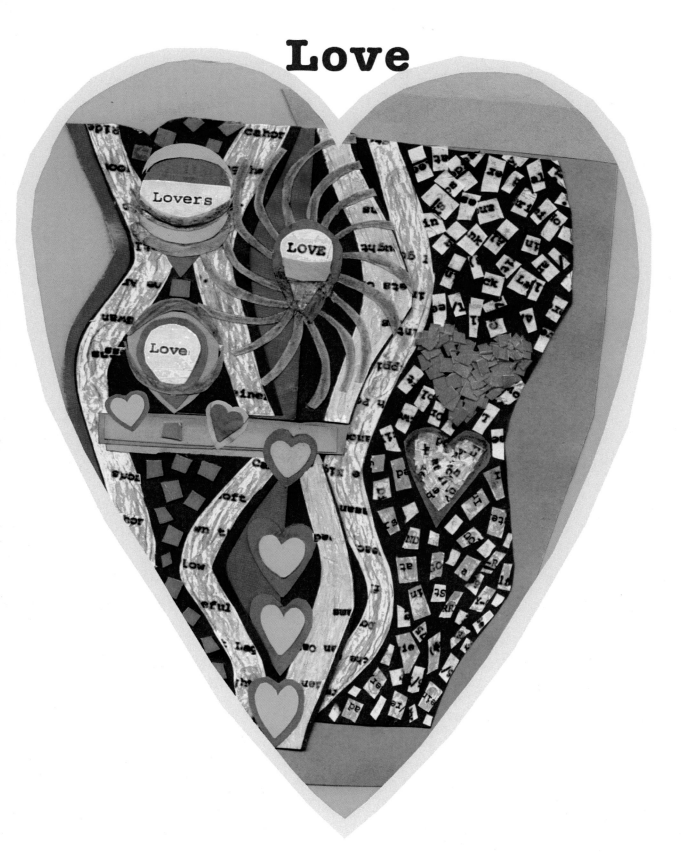

Recent Discoveries

When these works were found
buried in a pile, we stopped the press
to include them.

Rose Shiva

She had long white hair,
a tiny oval face and
dark doe-shaped eyes.
From the darkness of those
gentle eyes came a great light
that killed me with warmth.

When its bloom is done,
the Rose rejoins the earth
from whence she sprang.
Falling at the feet of
a New Leaf and a New Bud,
She nourishes them.
She becomes them.

The candle lit when she died
has a long white flame.
On the seventh day of its life
when the body of the candle
has been consumed, no longer visible,
the flame warmth will have passed on to me,
just as her Soul-Energy will pass
through the darkness of loss
into the light of life and
become part of my Soul-Energy.
In death as in life,
from darkness springs light.

To My Grandmother

I told my friend that
if you were Inuit,
when your time came
your bones weary
and your mind wandering,
visiting far-off places
many mountain peaks away,
high above the snow-covered
land you had always known,
when your teeth could no
longer soften seal gut or
chew it into sewing threads,
when you could no longer
hear the owl hoot
or lovers sing,
when your eyes refused to
focus but saw only a faint
whiteness glowing about you,
the Eskimos would have

taken you out to the
Great White Wonderland.
They would have made you
a powdery snow down bed,
and tucked you in
with love.

I told my friend
that the Plains Indians
would have lifted you up high,
set you atop their world
onto a holy platform that
you might see into the clouds
and your soul step
into the heavens.

I told my friend
that in Tibet the monks and I
would have chanted
a mellow OM
Pass word for you
to find the Way
to open the door in peace
and reach out to eternity.

I told my friend
that in America
when Grandmother walks through
her childhood haunts
and cannot find her friends,
when her roots begin to wither
and fall away,
when her life-blood is
slowly seeping into Mother Earth,
she is put in a Home
where they attach her to
Machines that pump her
full of Plastic Life until
she dies a modern death.

And, I told my friend,
I would not lead
My Grandmother into
Siberia's Wasteland where
she could not rest her aging limbs,
a place where Emptiness reigns
and no flowers like my Rose
can bloom, for Pluto and Persephone
have been exiled, ex-communicated.

My Grandmother lives at home
I said,
what better place could there be?
No, I would not call on Poe's
Dr. Mesmer
to keep her on. That same day,
She passed away.
I cannot say she suffered and
I cannot say she was unhappy.

I will tell my friend
that she is gone from me
I will tell my friend
that I am sad.

SHORT ONES

Mirror Mirror on the Wall

If I put on lipstick
will our lips stick?
Will it be for ever?

Joy

The rain no longer reigned
the Sun began to shine
&
all in all it
Snowed
me!

76

Night

The Moon Rose
Evergreen Higher
As the Sun Purpled
and Sank,
Hoots and calls
Arose with
Black cup-poured Sanka
As steaming hot
the night
came.

Margie's beloved bird
Cockles

Gifts

Give a personal appearance by a local poet.
Gift certificates - good for one reading.
I will create a serious, spiritual and/or fanciful event for you.
Celebrations can become once-in-a-lifetime happenings.

I will act as a non-legal priest for declaration of love/marriage.
I will read love poems to you and your loving-one on your anniversary,
birthdays or holy day of your choosing.
Maybe you can't have violins serenading your lover,
or orchids delivered to your restaurant table,
however, you can have your very own poet in person!

Let a couple of rare birds entertain you: arrange an appearance
of myself and the lovely white cockatoo.

Margie's List of Poems

Title

- Rendezvouz by Dawn
- Operation #II : Atlas
- Snow Drops
- Candle
- Hospitals
- Escape
- Raggedy Ann
- Essence
- Spring
- Cherry-In-Blossom-Tree
- Bon Voyage
- Dreams
- Fishing
- Rapunzel
- The Oyster
- Knave of Hearts
- Tomorrow
- To My Grandmother
- Rose
- Untitled (or) Bogged Down.
- Horizons
- Anniversary
- Night Voyage
- Orgchasm
- Moving
- Shadow Woman
- Aladdin's Lamp
- Impressions
- What Does It Matter cloud catchers
- The Handicapped Hunch
- Orbiting
- Red Hot Roses
- Candle Mass
- Death
- Surprise

Title

- Night
- Communication
- Mary Had a Little Lamb
- Depression
- Joy
- Of Doom
- Black-Out
- Eclipse Through an Oval Window
- In Rhyme nor Reason
- It's In Sane
- Through An Eye of Love
- The Birth
- You My Friend
- How's That for Flying
- House Boat In China
- I am a Baker Poet
- Ditty Do
- The Banjo Player
- Raindrops
- Teardrops
- Sea Lion
- Revlon Revelation
- Inside the Golden Flute
- Water Can
- The Tacky Attack
- Winning is the Game
- Ingrained Sequence
- Country Cabin Blues
- Hospital Visit
- Ode to Errol Flynn
- On a Winter's Day
- Castle in the Sky
- Nocturnal Visits
- Six Sweet Rolls
- Morphine, Plutonic Prince of the Under Ground

I Have a Friend
Sleeping Alone
Passengers
Lunar Eclipse
Wet Dream
Meditating
In the Tea Cup
Candelabra Cadabra
Conjunction
It Is All With In
Pumpkin Pie
Moon Womb
Light Tide Out
Peter's Skip Rope Sunset
San Francisco Sunset
The Snow Goose Ride
Later
My Poems
Flying Above San Diego
Landing in San Francisco
I Lift My Head
Monarch
The Shy Volcano
Cockatoo
An Indian Brave
Goddess of the Marsh
Birth Pains
Mosses (*) (Poem 104)
At Dusk Nissho
I Search the Skies
Earth Quake
Ten Drops
Cockatoo
Reindeer Moss
I saw the Sun

The Kiss
Solunar Corona
The Three Eyes
The Issue or The Issuance
BonVoyage in Sanskrit (or)
On Climbing the Mountain
Yin Yang Revolutions
On Our Way
My Soul Aches
Thought Travels title: 4/27/96
After the Wash
My Friend the Humming Bird
Transition
        Rabbit
     County Fair
  Kashmir
My Muse
The Pied Piper & I
The Rape of the Valley
In the Jungle
The Mask
Memories of the Sixth Grade
I am the Silver-Caped Wave
I feel like Cracked Crab
The Black Apple Seed
Lighter Than Air
Abra Cadabra
The Secret
The Pyramid of Life
Midday at The Pool

*In Margie's hand —
titles of some
of her many poems*

81

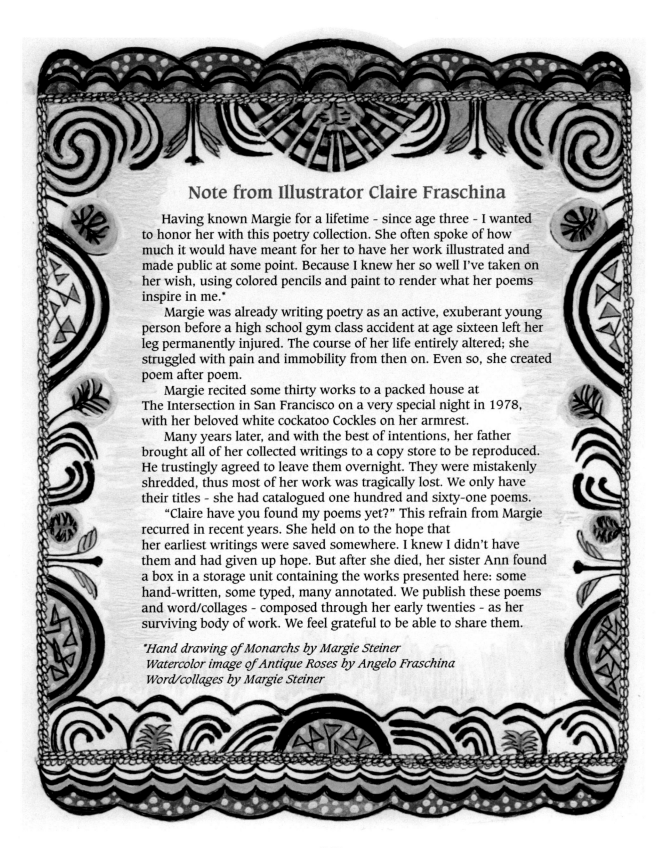

Note from Illustrator Claire Fraschina

Having known Margie for a lifetime - since age three - I wanted to honor her with this poetry collection. She often spoke of how much it would have meant for her to have her work illustrated and made public at some point. Because I knew her so well I've taken on her wish, using colored pencils and paint to render what her poems inspire in me.*

Margie was already writing poetry as an active, exuberant young person before a high school gym class accident at age sixteen left her leg permanently injured. The course of her life entirely altered; she struggled with pain and immobility from then on. Even so, she created poem after poem.

Margie recited some thirty works to a packed house at The Intersection in San Francisco on a very special night in 1978, with her beloved white cockatoo Cockles on her armrest.

Many years later, and with the best of intentions, her father brought all of her collected writings to a copy store to be reproduced. He trustingly agreed to leave them overnight. They were mistakenly shredded, thus most of her work was tragically lost. We only have their titles - she had catalogued one hundred and sixty-one poems.

"Claire have you found my poems yet?" This refrain from Margie recurred in recent years. She held on to the hope that her earliest writings were saved somewhere. I knew I didn't have them and had given up hope. But after she died, her sister Ann found a box in a storage unit containing the works presented here: some hand-written, some typed, many annotated. We publish these poems and word/collages - composed through her early twenties - as her surviving body of work. We feel grateful to be able to share them.

Hand drawing of Monarchs by Margie Steiner
Watercolor image of Antique Roses by Angelo Fraschina
Word/collages by Margie Steiner

Especial thanks to our layout *meister* Philip DiLernia for outstanding teamwork in this and earlier Sunbath Studios publications. He wears many hats here, from cover creation, to photo detailing, color calligraphy, type design, Photoshop expertise, extra embellishment and illustration of the original Intersection building on Union Street. His sincere desire to make reading Margie's work pleasurable is evident in his precision and passion. Margie would surely feel grateful, as we do.

Natalie Galli and Claire Fraschina

DiLERNIA 2020

"Every successful creative must have a third eye. As always, as in this case, my partner & endearing wife, Lienne-Brent DiLernia."
Philip DiLernia

Made in the USA
Columbia, SC
14 May 2022